WORKBOOK

4

ENSINO FUNDAMENTAL
ANOS INICIAIS

RENATO MENDES CURTO JÚNIOR
ANNA CAROLINA GUIMARÃES
CIBELE MENDES

CONTENTS

UNIT 1
A special school day _____ 3

UNIT 2
Sports and health _____ 9

UNIT 3
A friend's visit _____ 11

UNIT 4
At the cafeteria _____ 14

UNIT 5
The fun visit to the museum _____ 20

UNIT 6
The music class _____ 24

UNIT 7
At the shopping mall _____ 28

UNIT 8
Different jobs _____ 30

UNIT 1

A SPECIAL SCHOOL DAY

1 Which school subjects do the images relate to?

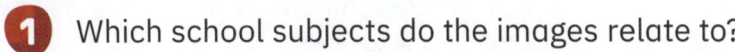

Math ● Language ● Art
English ● Science ● History
Geography ● Physical Education (P.E.)

a)  _____

e)  _____

b)  _____

f)  _____

c) 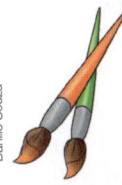 _____

g)  _____

d)  _____

h)  _____

THREE 3

2 Which preposition of place does each image represent?

> At • On • In front of
> In • Near • Between

a)

_____

b)

_____

c)

_____

d)

_____

e)

_____

f)

_____

3 Fill in the gaps with the correct articles.

a) _____ pet
b) _____ onion
c) _____ car
d) _____ river
e) _____ elbow
f) _____ egg

4 Complete the following school timetable with the information about your schedules and the subjects you study at school. Use the words from the box.

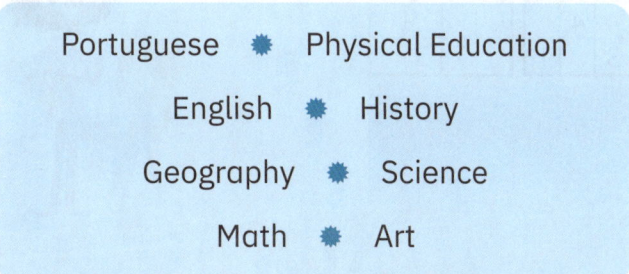
Portuguese * Physical Education
English * History
Geography * Science
Math * Art

School Timetable

Time	Monday	Tuesday	Wednesday	Thursday	Friday	Saturday

5 Write the names of the children under the image that represents the activities they like to do.

* **Rosa**: She loves singing American songs.
* **Mônica**: She loves numbers and logic puzzles.
* **Daniela**: She loves drawing and painting.
* **Felipe**: He loves sports.

a)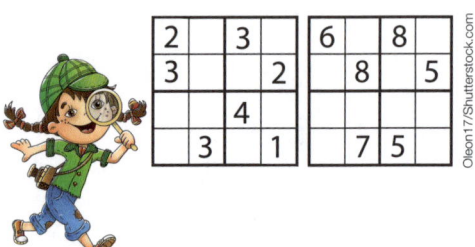

_____

c)

_____

b)

_____

d)

_____

6 Now, complete the sentences with these subjects: Art, Math, Physical Education, and Music.

a) Rosa's favorite subject is _____.

b) Mônica's favorite subject is _____.

c) Daniela's favorite subject is _____.

d) Felipe's favorite subject is _____.

7 Draw the objects in the **correct** column. Follow the example.

- Umbrella
- Pear
- Apple
- Ball
- Dog
- Eraser
- Ant
- Duck
- Orange
- Pencil

A	An
	 **an** umbrella

8 Complete with A or AN.

a)
_____ bike

d)
_____ umbrella

b)
_____ teacher

e)
_____ car

c)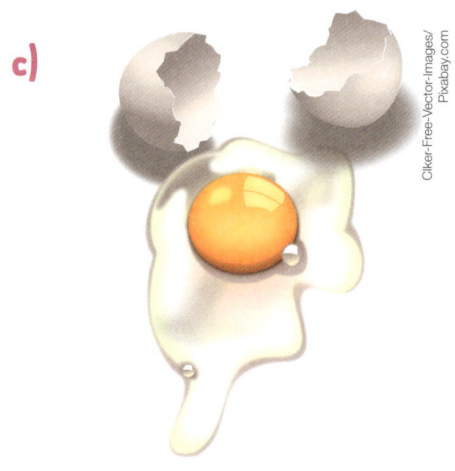
_____ egg

f)
_____ eraser

UNIT 2
SPORTS AND HEALTH

1 What sport do they practice?

a)  _____

b)  _____

c)  _____

d)  _____

e)  _____

f)  _____

g)  _____

h)  _____

i)  _____

j)  _____

NINE 9

2 Complete the sentences with the name of the objects and the correct possessive pronoun.

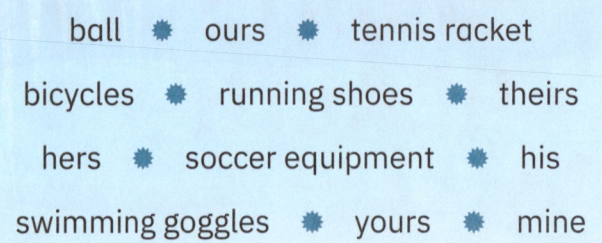

ball • ours • tennis racket
bicycles • running shoes • theirs
hers • soccer equipment • his
swimming goggles • yours • mine

a)

That _____ is _____.

d)

That _____ is _____.

b)

These _____ are _____.

e)

These _____ are _____.

c)

These _____ are _____.

f)

That _____ is _____.

UNIT 3
A FRIEND'S VISIT

1 Complete the sentences with **this** or **that**.

a)
_____ is my favorite book!

c)
_____ is my ball.

b)
_____ is my bike!

d)
_____ is my backpack.

2 Match the demonstrative pronouns with their correct definitions.

a) This   ✸ a person or a thing, far.

b) That   ✸ a person or a thing, near.

ELEVEN 11

3 Complete the sentences with **these** or **those**.

a)
_____ are my books from school!

c)
_____ are business buildings.

b)
_____ are my kites!

d)
_____ are my dolls.

e)
_____ are our backpacks.

4 Choose the correct definition for each demonstrative pronoun.

a) These
- ☐ people or things, near.
- ☐ people or things, far.

b) Those
- ☐ people or things, near.
- ☐ people or things, far.

5 Match the action verbs to the pictures.

a) to run

Armation/Shutterstock.com

b) to jump

Colorfuel Studio/Shutterstock.com

c) to sing

yatate/Shutterstock.com

d) to eat

Sketch Master/Shutterstock.com

e) to sleep

Colorfuel Studio/ Shutterstock.com

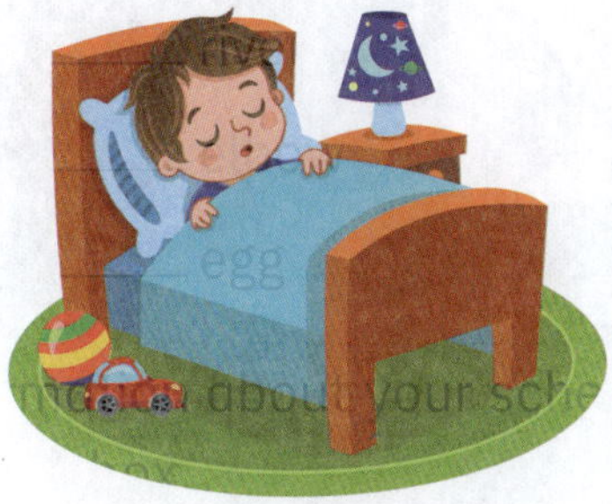

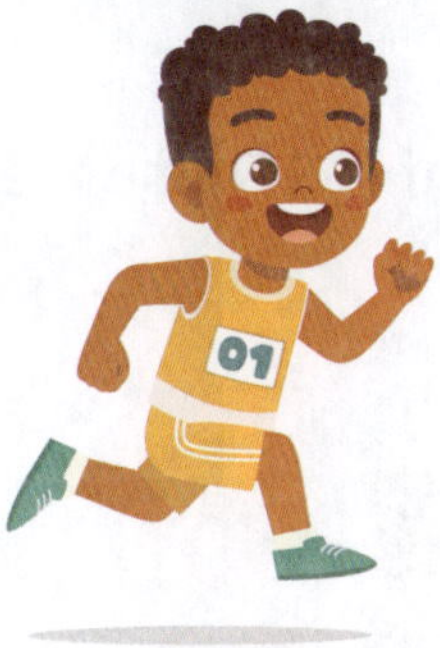

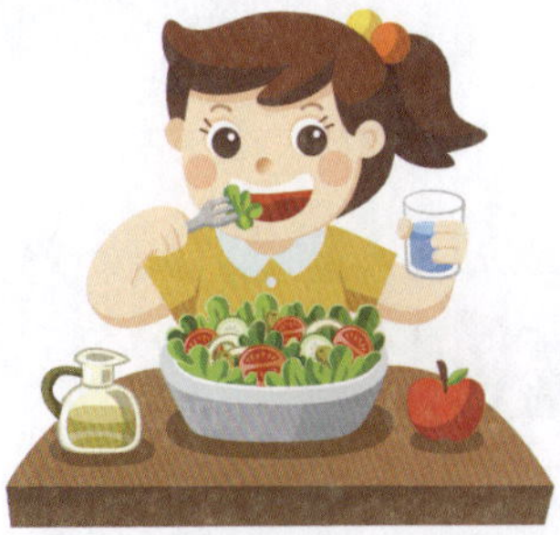

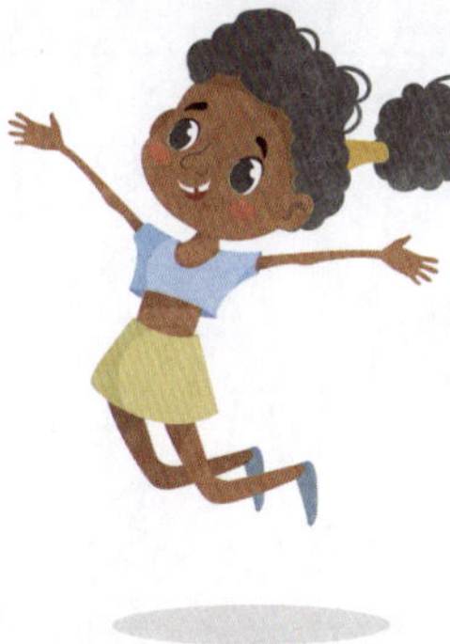

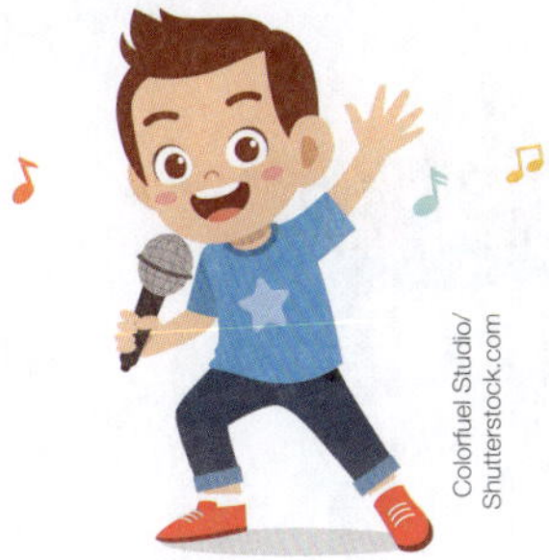

UNIT 4
AT THE CAFETERIA

1 What are they? Name them correctly.

a)
_____

b)
_____

c)
_____

d)
_____

e)
_____

f)
_____

g)
_____

h)
_____

i)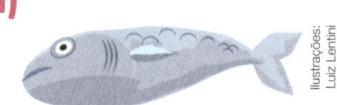
_____

j)
_____

k)
_____

l)
_____

2 Organize the food items into the correct categories. Some of them fit in more than one category.

- Juice
- Steak
- Tea
- Cheese
- Pie
- Chicken
- Beans
- Hot dog
- Fish
- Vegetables
- Cookies
- Fruits

Breakfast	Lunch	Dinner

3 Mark the healthy food with 1 and the junk food with 2. Then find their names in the word search.

Y	E	V	G	U	Q	D	X	U	T	O	P	S	A	D
N	M	A	S	D	F	T	R	A	T	I	O	U	B	E
H	O	T	*	D	O	G	A	B	C	D	E	F	G	B
L	M	N	O	P	Q	R	S	O	D	A	X	Z	K	A
A	A	E	I	O	U	B	C	D	E	F	G	H	J	N
F	R	E	N	C	H	*	F	R	I	E	S	B	B	A
I	E	A	Z	X	C	V	B	N	M	A	S	D	F	N
J	F	I	S	H	W	E	R	H	U	I	O	P	Y	A
A	B	C	D	Y	T	T	R	A	T	J	K	L	M	E

16   SIXTEEN

4 Form sentences using **would like** and the given information.

a) Camila/ some fruit salad.
_____

b) Peter/ a hamburger with french fries.
_____

c) Anna/ a vegetable salad and a steak.
_____

d) Ted/ a chocolate pie.
_____

5 What would you like to do? Unscramble and match the sentences to the pictures.

a) like – eat – to – I'd – pizza
_____

b) would – go – the – to – beach – like – She – to
_____

c) drink – They'd – to – water – like
_____

d) would – I – travel – to – like
_____

SEVENTEEN **17**

6 Let's make a pictionary (a dictionary of pictures)! Select words related to **food** and make a pictionary with pictures and the names of different types of food. Use the images below as an example. Don't forget to organize the items in alphabetical order.

7 What is there in the fruit bowl? Observe the image and mark the **correct** sentences.

a) There are two apples.

b) There are some bananas.

c) There are three oranges.

d) There is one apple.

e) There is a banana.

f) There are some grapes.

g) There is only one grape.

h) There is an orange.

8 Match the food and the drink to the **correct** pictures.

a) apple

b) muffin

c) water

d) orange juice

e) sandwich

f) pizza

g) fruit salad

h) banana

i) milk

UNIT 5
THE FUN VISIT TO THE MUSEUM

1 Complete the text with the correct information.

> Art Museum
> field trip
> because there is an art research for the school project
> June 15th
> Art teacher and the class 4C

Dear parents,

There is a _____ with the _____ to the _____ on _____.

We are doing this field trip _____.

2 Write the numbers in full.

a) 100 – _____

b) 91 – _____

c) 82 – _____

d) 73 – _____

e) 64 – _____

f) 55 – _____

g) 46 – _____

h) 37 – _____

i) 28 – _____

j) 19 – _____

3 Choose the best option.

a) Italy
- [ ] When
- [ ] Where
- [ ] Who

b) April 2nd
- [ ] When
- [ ] Why
- [ ] Who

c) Beyoncé
- [ ] Where
- [ ] What
- [ ] Who

d) My books.
- [ ] Where
- [ ] What
- [ ] Who

e) Because she loves fruit salad.
- [ ] When
- [ ] Where
- [ ] Why

4 Write the numbers in the numeric form.

a) ninety-two – _____

b) eighty-one – _____

c) seventy-two – _____

d) sixty-three – _____

e) fifty-five – _____

f) forty-seven – _____

g) thirty-four – _____

h) twenty-nine – _____

i) seventeen – _____

j) eight – _____

5 Pedro and Clara are talking at school. Complete their conversation with **who**, **what** or **where**.

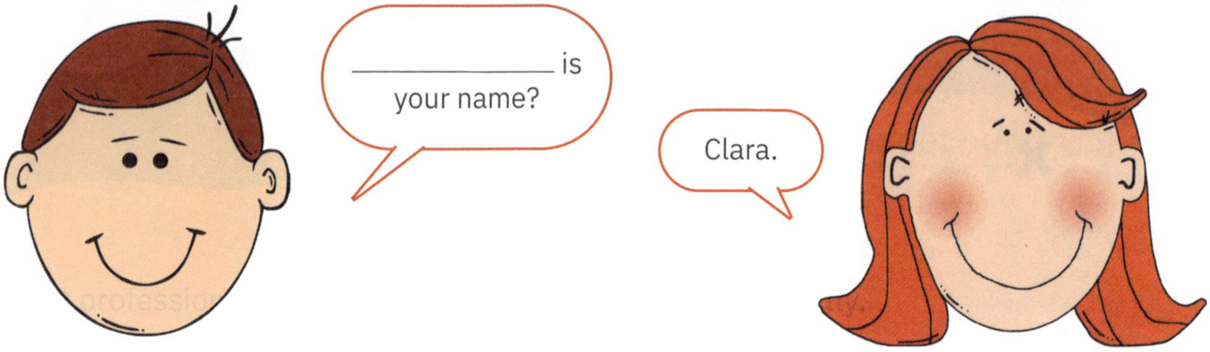

_____ is your name?

Clara.

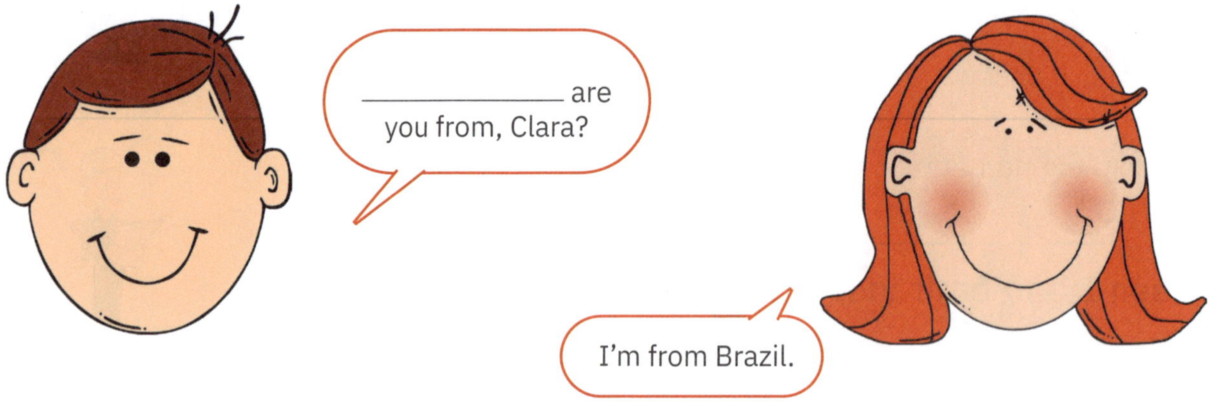

_____ are you from, Clara?

I'm from Brazil.

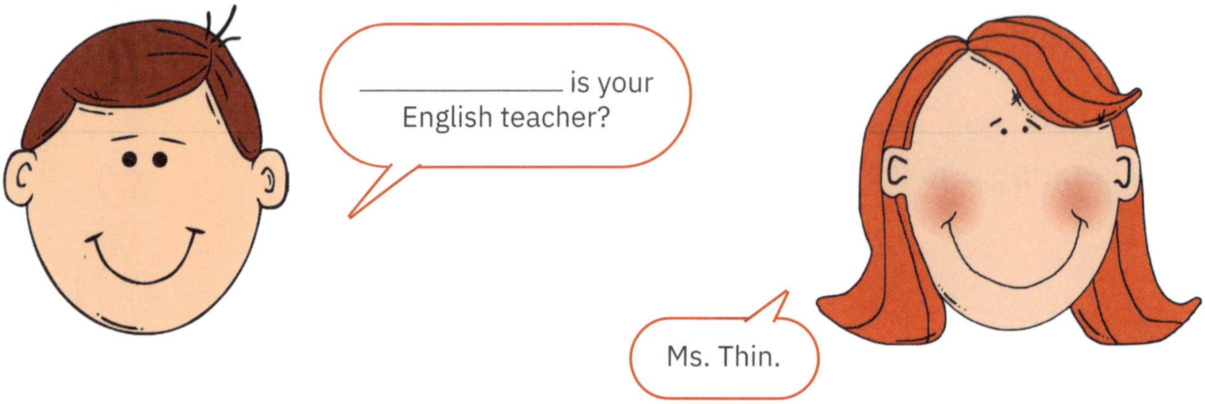

_____ is your English teacher?

Ms. Thin.

6 Circle the **correct** pronoun to complete the questions.

a) _____ is your favorite singer?

| WHAT | WHERE | WHEN | WHO |

b) _____ is your brother's name?

| WHAT | WHERE | WHEN | WHO |

c) _____ do you study? In the morning or in the afternoon?

| WHAT | WHERE | WHEN | WHO |

d) _____ do you live?

| WHAT | WHERE | WHEN | WHO |

e) _____ is your best friend?

| WHAT | WHERE | WHEN | WHO |

f) _____ is your mom now?

| WHAT | WHERE | WHEN | WHO |

g) _____ is your dad's birthday?

| WHAT | WHERE | WHEN | WHO |

h) _____ kind of music do you like?

| WHAT | WHERE | WHEN | WHO |

UNIT 6

THE MUSIC CLASS

1 What music style do they represent?

a)
_____

b)
_____

2 Choose the **correct** option to complete each sentence.

a) He _____ my best friend.

   (**a**) is   (**b**) are   (**c**) am

b) They _____ soccer players.

   (**a**) is   (**b**) are   (**c**) am

c) Peter _____ very sad.

   (**a**) is   (**b**) are   (**c**) am

d) It _____ a beautiful day.

   (**a**) is   (**b**) are   (**c**) am

e) I _____ a good student.

   (**a**) is   (**b**) are   (**c**) am

3 Complete the sentences with the correct form of the verb **to be.**

a) I _____ late for the music class.

b) You _____ my best friend's brother.

c) She _____ my aunt Claire.

d) He _____ our Language teacher.

e) It _____ Susana's cat.

f) We _____ a happy family.

g) You _____ great as a soccer team.

h) Taylor and Clay _____ best friends.

i) Janet, Dulce and I _____ late for the Science class.

j) Carl _____ my grandfather.

k) Helen _____ my little sister.

l) I _____ hungry.

4 What musical instrument is it?

a)
- ☐ Guitar
- ☐ Drums

b)
- ☐ Flute
- ☐ Drums

c)
- ☐ Harmonica
- ☐ Violin

d)
- ☐ Guitar
- ☐ Flute

e)
- ☐ Saxophone
- ☐ Violin

f)
- ☐ Piano
- ☐ Violin

g)
- ☐ Tambourine
- ☐ Drums

h)
- ☐ Accordion
- ☐ Tambourine

i)
- ☐ Guitar
- ☐ Harmonica

5 Complete the names of these musical instruments. Write the missing vowels.

Example:

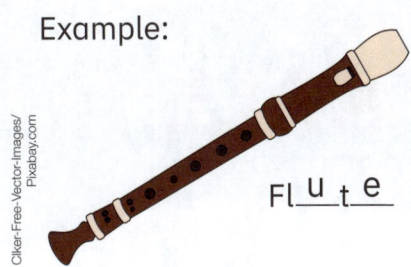

Fl_u_t_e_

a)

Gu__t__r

b)

Dr__ms

c)

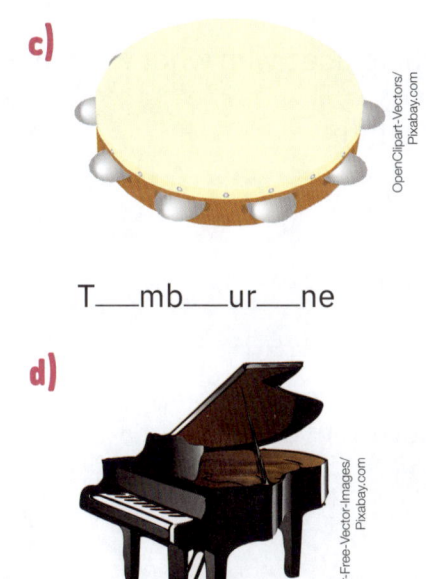

T__mb__ur__ne

d)

P__an__

6 Which instruments above can we use for these music styles? Complete the lists.

Samba	Classical music	Rock

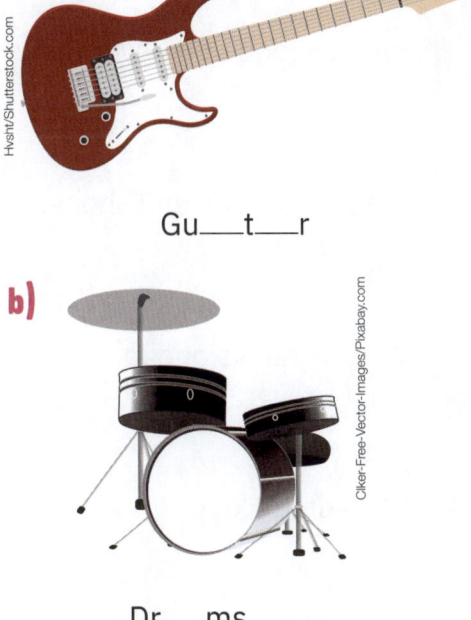

UNIT 7 AT THE SHOPPING MALL

1 Match the places with what we can do there.

a) Bookstore   ✸ We buy food and beverages.

b) Cinema   ✸ We buy clothes and shoes.

c) Department store   ✸ We buy books and magazines.

d) Food court   ✸ We watch plays.

e) Theater   ✸ We watch movies.

2 Unscramble the letters.

a) serds: _____

b) sroebokot: _____

c) svmoie: _____

d) plfi-lofps: _____

e) nptsa: _____

f) hoses: _____

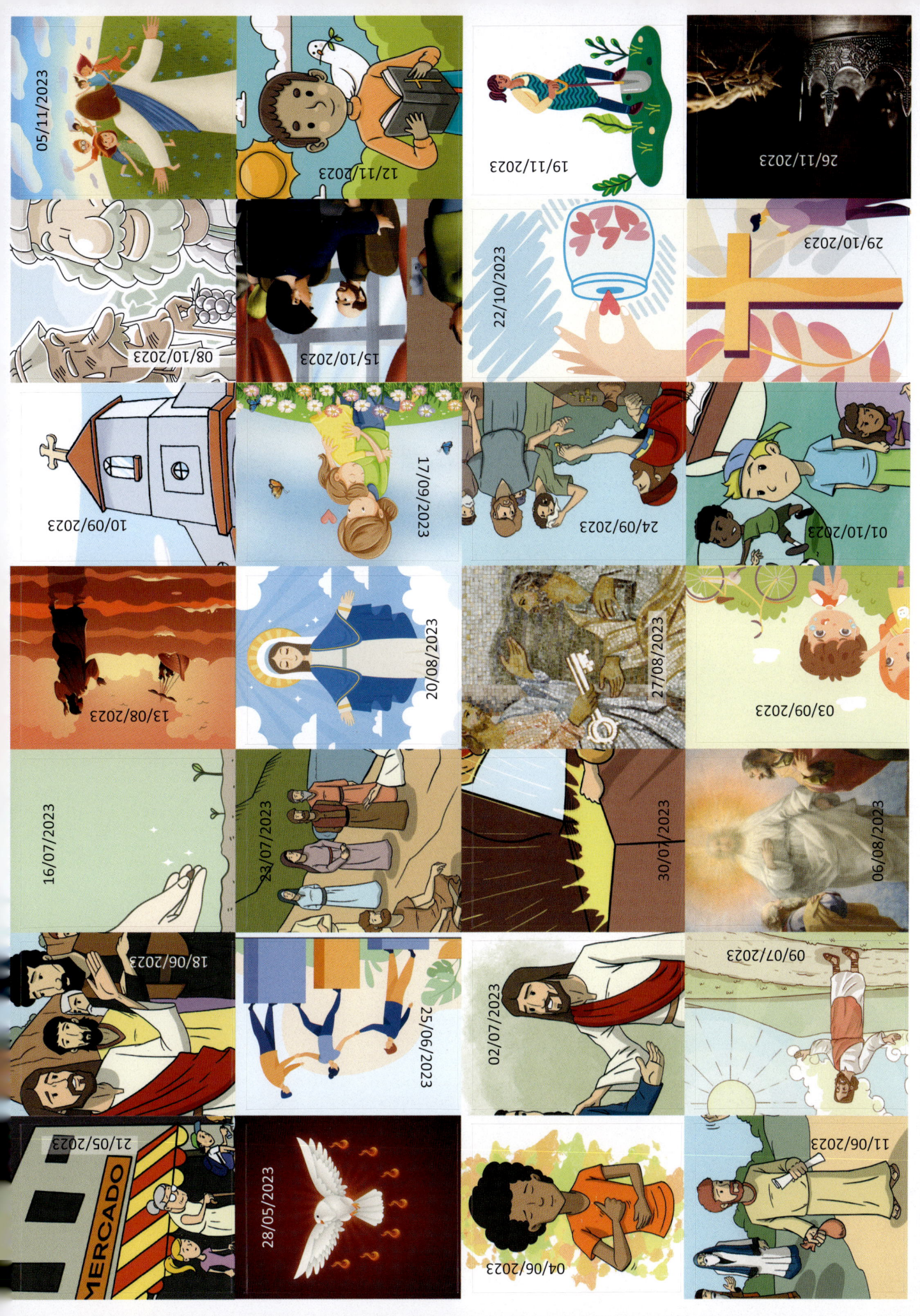

3 What is this? Name the clothing items and find them in the word search.

a) _____
b) _____
c) _____
d) _____
e) _____
f) _____
g) _____
h) _____
i) _____
j) _____

H	D	R	E	S	S	G	A	C	S	O	C	K	S	I
S	M	N	O	H	Q	S	T	-	S	H	I	R	T	Y
N	A	E	I	O	U	C	S	E	F	G	H	P	L	L
E	R	E	N	E	H	F	S	I	E	S	B	P	E	S
A	E	A	Z	S	C	B	K	M	A	H	D	A	X	A
K	K	L	Ç	Q	W	R	I	U	I	O	P	N	T	N
E	B	C	D	Y	T	R	R	T	J	R	L	T	U	D
R	Q	R	E	B	S	G	T	V	X	T	K	S	C	A
S	S	X	D	P	G	H	J	H	J	S	L	C	W	L
A	E	A	S	H	I	R	T	W	S	B	T	P	Y	S

UNIT 8
DIFFERENT JOBS

1 What profession do they represent? Name each one correctly.

a)
_____

b)
_____

c)
_____

d)
_____

e)
_____

f)
_____

g)
_____

h)
_____

2 Match the podium positions to their ordinal numbers and write them in full.

2
1
3

YummyBuum/Shutterstock.com

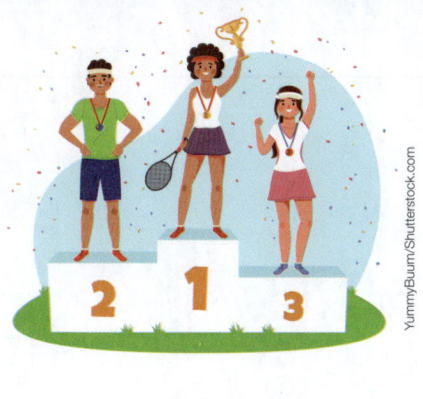

2nd ____________________ 3rd ____________________ 1st ____________________

3 Complete the crossword with ordinal numbers.

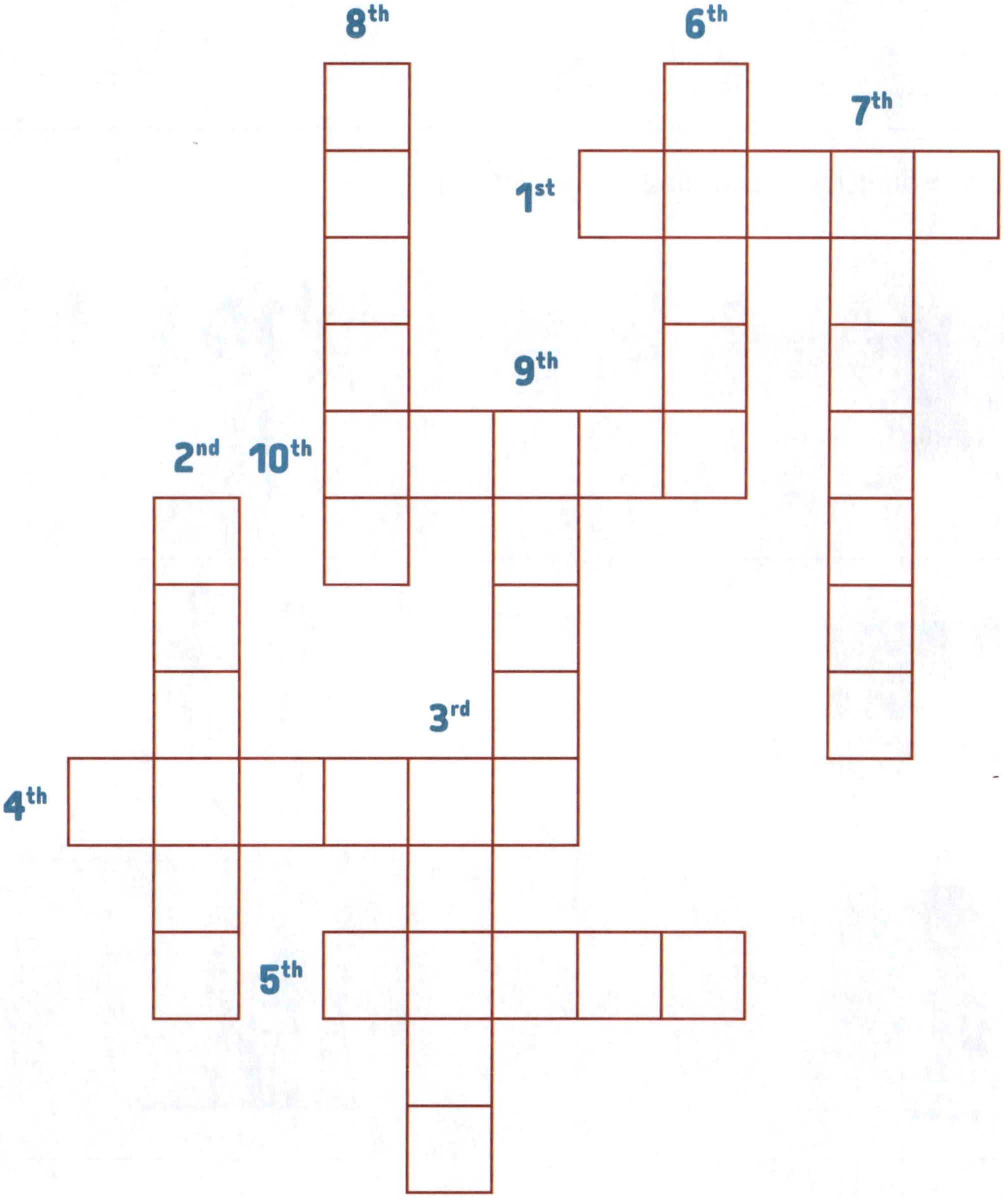
8th
6th
7th
1st
9th
2nd
10th
3rd
4th
5th

4 Find these professions in the word search: journalist, teacher, musician, doctor and engineer.

Z	J	O	U	R	N	A	L	I	S	T	V
I	O	J	S	W	H	J	U	S	S	K	D
M	U	S	I	C	I	A	N	G	M	B	O
B	X	G	K	J	B	B	S	E	D	S	C
E	N	G	I	N	E	E	R	A	W	W	T
M	X	C	G	X	P	I	K	Q	K	B	O
X	S	A	R	F	T	E	A	C	H	E	R

5 Name the professions according to the pictures.

a)
_____

d)
_____

b)
_____

e)
_____

c)
_____

f)
_____